Craigslist Money Making

Table of Content

Introduction

Chapter 1

Earning a Living from Craigslist

Chapter 2

How to Use Craigslist in

Order to Earn a Profit

Chapter 3

Some Tips to Help You Get Started

Chapter 4

Ways of Making Money through Craigslist

Chapter 5

How to Post Your Advertisement on Craigslist

Conclusion

Introduction

Today, Craigslist is one of the most well known of all online urban communities on the web. It allows people to place free classified adverts relating to various subjects, as well as having forums where people can discuss various topics.

Craigslist was founded by Craig Newmark from the San Francisco Bay Area in 1995. Then it became incorporated in 1999. Since its incorporation as of November 2006, there were over 450 cities where a Craigslist has been established.

The business now operates with a team of 24 people, and the only way they make any revenue today is through the job adverts paid for in selected cities around the States. Ads placed by companies in the San Francisco Bay Area cost $75, while those placed by companies or businesses in New York, Los Angeles, San Diego, Boston, Seattle and Washington DC will cost them $25 for each advert placed. Also today, a real estate broker will need to pay $10 for any apartment listings they place on Craigslist for New York.

Today, this site is receiving over 500,000 new job listings each month, and so makes it one of the top job boards in the world today. The classified adverts that are placed on this site range from more traditional ones where people are able to buy and sell goods, to community announcements…even personal adverts or erotic services are being provided through this site.

In its early years, most of the postings placed on the Craigslist were submitted by its founder, and were generally dealing with social events that were of interest to software and internet developers who lived and worked in the San Francisco area.

However, as more and more people learned about this site, it began to grow at an extremely high rate. Certainly, as more and more subscribers began to use the site, so the number of postings to it also began to grow as well.

Certainly those people who were looking to fill technical positions found this list to be a great way of reaching those with the necessary skills that they were searching for. Because of this, the demand for a section dedicated to jobs was created. Plus, the demand by the lists' users for more categories to be able to post and search under also began to grow as well. It was at this time that more and more of the sites users asked for a web interface to be set up.

It was through the help of various volunteers and contractors that such a website user interface was created for each different mailing list category to be found on the list. As the domain required a name, Craig Newman first registered "craigslist.org" and then followed it up later on with "craigslist.com", which helped to prevent the name from being used for some other purpose.

Certainly if you were to search on Craigslist today, the most popular of all the forums is the one known as the "Erotic Forum". This forum is now often used by law enforcement agencies for decoy operations, and Craigslist co-operates in any way it can to help prevent its users from selling drugs, sex or stolen property through its listings.

Through this book, we are going to look at the ways in which a person can legally profit from using Craigslist. We will discuss the ways in which a person can set up a business in their own home, and which will provide them with a chance to earn an additional income or their main form of income.

Chapter 1

Earning a Living from Craigslist

You may find it difficult to believe, but it is easily and possible for someone to earn a living from Craigslist. As more and more people have begun to realize, there are a number of different opportunities available to those who are willing to put in a little hard work so they can earn a living online.

For beginners, it is important that you have learned everything that there is that one needs to know about online communities like Craigslist. Plus, learning how to market themselves, as well as their products or skills, to those who might be interested in what they have to offer, has now become business.

The great thing about offering your services online, compared to providing them in the more conventional manner, is that you are setting no cap on just how much you can earn. But using this method does not mean that you will earn lots, mainly it will depend on what you are offering to others.

There are 2 ways in which a person can earn a living through Craigslist. They may decide to offer their services or products in the following ways:-

2. As an independent contractor who provides their services to a customer on a contract basis.

3. Or they offer their products or services to others in the same way that a small business

owner would.

However, there are many individuals who are using Craigslist in order to find a job (and thus, build their business).

In this particular chapter of our book, we will look at the way independent contractors and small business owners can utilize the services that Craigslist provides to their subscribers.

Independent Contractors

This is an excellent place for such people to offer their services, as well as being able to respond to adverts placed by others. As more and more companies, both big and small, look to outsourcing certain sections of their business, then there are plenty of individuals who have suddenly realized the advantages to be gained from these outsourcing opportunities as and when they arise.

These people are able to place adverts for the services that they provide, as well as being given the chance to respond to those adverts that they see where companies are seeking employees on a contract basis to provide the services that they can offer.

Today, you will find a section on Craigslist which is dedicated to offering services to their subscribers. Under this section, you will find various sub sections where a number of different services are now being offered. So the great thing is that you, as an independent contractor, are able to place your posting under the category that is most appropriate to the service that you can provide, and this will reach those that you are intending to target.

Plus, if you can not find a category that provides for your particular service, then you can also use the small business advertisement section in order for you to advertise your services. But you may find that it is a little more difficult for you to reach your target audience through the use of this category on Craigslist.

Many of those independent contractors who advertise their services on Craigslist have found that they have gained more business because they have responded to advertisements placed by those people, businesses and companies who are looking for contract based employees.

When searching for a position using Craigslist, a contractor can start their search by typing in a particular location. Then they can start to browse through the various different jobs that come up for that location by category.

The best and easiest way for anyone to find a contract job on this site is through the use of the search feature and by placing a tick in the contract box, which will then ensure that this term is used as part of the search requirements you request of the system. By doing this, you are assured that every position result provided to you will only be ones that are of a contract nature.

Small Business Owners

They can utilize this list in order that they may reach a much larger target audience, which will then help their business to grow. There are a couple of advantages to be had from using Craigslist, and these are as follows:-

4. It allows the small business owner to post an advert in the most appropriate category on the site. This can be extremely effective, as it now receives more than 4 billion page views each month, so there is potential for any small business to be able to reach a much larger and more potentially lucrative audience than they would using any other method of advertisement.

5. It allows them to use the discussion forums within Craigslist, which can help them to generate even greater profits for their business. But they should be wary of how they use promotional postings on these forums, as some people may mistake them for being spam. There is a very distinct way in which a person can post information regarding their business to these forums so that they are found informative by the readers, instead of it looking like spam, which is solely used to promote a business and nothing else.

Unfortunately, those businesses who use spamming are not only likely to find that they get overlooked by those in the forum, but may well find that Craigslist moderators will actually delete whatever it is that they have posted. They could even take much more severe action against that business, banning them from using their listings altogether.

Chapter 2

How to Use Craigslist in Order to Earn a Profit

The great thing is that Craigslist can be used in a number of different ways for a person to earn a profit from it. Certainly some of the most popular ways that people are now using this particular site is to advertise their product or services, to meet people or just to find a job.

In this particular chapter, we will take a closer look at three ways a person can use Craigslist.

Advertising

This is probably one of the best ways for a person to utilize what Craigslist has to offer. Certainly, many people who are looking to make a profit from either a product, or service that they are selling, will turn to this particular site for one of two reasons.

The two main reasons why people are so keen to use Craigslist is the costs to advertise (extremely affordable) and they know that this site comes with a large pre-existing audience.

In fact, the only charges that Craigslist makes when it comes to advertising on this particular site, is for postings relating to job advertisements, and only in certain market areas, and for housing advertisements that have been placed in one city (New York). So advertising your product or service on this site is actually free.

Because Craigslist is now receiving around 10 million visitors to it each month, and these are then generating around about 4 billion page views a month, you will find that, by placing an advertisement here, it will help you to reach a much larger target audience than you would normally do through other methods of advertising your business (and, as already mentioned, at a much more affordable price for your advertisements).

Meet People

Today, this section of Craigslist is devoted to providing individuals with the chance to post or read advertisements from others that are seeking plutonic or romantic relationships, no matter what their sexual orientation is.

However, only those over the age of 18 are allowed access to this particular section of Craigslist. Plus, other restrictions have been placed upon this section above the normal restrictions required of those who set up websites on the internet today.

One of these restrictions, and probably the most important of all, is that you may not impersonate someone else when placing an advertising posting at this site.

As the site has a number of different discussion forums available to its subscribers, it provides people with a chance to meet like minded souls.

The diversity of users is part of what makes Craigslist such an attractive place for advertising. There are sure to be others interested in the subject of your product or service…you simply have to be able to find them.

Finding Jobs

Many people who have come to Craigslist are often searching for a new job, or looking for a change in their career. This section of the site is quite extensive, and all jobs posted are broken down into various different categories.

By doing this, it makes the search for a particular position much easier for the user to find. Plus, the search features on this site allow the user to search for a job by using particular words or phrases.

They can also search for those jobs by using a certain set of criteria in relation to the job that they are interested in.

They can look for things such as contract positions, internships, part time, as well as full time positions, and those positions available in non profit organizations.

This section of the site also allows the user to post their CV (resume) for consideration. It is not as well organized as the rest of the site, but those who know how to write a CV which is going to catch a potential employer's eye, will do well using this section of the Craigslist.

Chapter 3

Some Tips to Help You get Started

You will soon discover that there are lots to be found on Craigslist, including both new, and second hand merchandise. But in this chapter, we will look at some tips which will help you to get started using this site, and help you to earn a profit.

The first thing that you need to do is create an account. Although not required, it is certainly beneficial, as posting items to the site is much simpler, and you will not need to wait for an email to arrive before you confirm that you want to submit a posting.

Open an Account

Also, by opening an account, it allows you to view and edit any listings you have posted, as well as view any of your old postings as well.

Next, you need to go the city where you are residing. Today, Craigslist offers listings in 300 cities in not just the USA, but in another 50 countries around the world also. All you need to do is key in your City name in order to go the Craigslist section for that area.

Include a Picture

When posting anything for sale to Craigslist, ensure that you include pictures. Many people miss this option, but you will see one when creating your listing that says "Add/Edit Images". All you need to do is have the images held either on your computer, or digital camera, and then you can upload them to Craigslist. Once uploaded, a copy of the image will be held on the system while the posting remains active.

Unfortunately, for those who do not include a picture in the listing, people will often ask if the seller has one (which means a lot more work and hassle emailing pictures to interested parties).

Also, they will generally move on to the next listing, or those that already have images with their posting or are willing to provide one when asked.

Look at other Craigslist Postings

If you look on the left hand side of the site, you will see a "best of" link, and these are the postings which have been nominated by the users as being interesting, funny or just down right crazy.

Unfortunately, none of these are endorsed by Craigslist, so be wary when looking at them, as they may not be appropriate for children to be looking at (or even some adults for that matter!).

However, by looking at them yourself, it may provide you with a way to show your service or product off to its best advantage, and help you to earn additional profit for your business.

Certainly, by keeping these tips in mind, you should be advertising your services or products much more effectively on Craigslist.

Chapter 4

Ways of Making Money through Craigslist

Craigslist is an online community where its users are able to buy or sell items, as well as looking for jobs or even meet and find new friends. It also allows its users to exchange information. This has now become the most complete site around the world, not just in the USA, offering free classified ads to those that peruse its pages.

Currently, Craigslist is averaging around 4 billion page views a month, and so it can offer those who want them, a wealth of financial opportunities, especially if they are willing to capitalize on this site's popularity. So if you are really keen to set up your own online business which can be run from the comfort of your own home, then it is advisable that you start looking for a service or product which you can advertise on Craigslist, and just see what results you achieve.

So let's take a look at some ways that you can make money through using Craigslist.

Sell products that are tangible on your Website

It can either be through a special offer or a sale. But all you need to do is go to the right category on Craigslist, and then submit a posting in relation to what it is you are offering for sale, along with the price that you are offering it at. Certainly, the better the deal you can provide to those visiting the site, then the more visitors it will bring to yours.

Selling products or services on eBay

Unfortunately, using this method in order to make money could be a problem if you do not have sufficient goods to sell. Plus, placing any sort of listing on eBay is going to cost you.

However, with Craigslist if you go to the "for sale" and then "free" section in various categories, you will be amazed at just what people are giving away. You can then get these goods for yourself, and if you want, start selling them on eBay, and make your profit from Craigslist in that way.

Selling Affiliate Products

If you are looking for a way to earn money at home by use of the internet, one way is to get involved in affiliate marketing. However, you will need to read the terms of service in relation to affiliate marketing on Craigslist, as this is not normally allowed. But there are ways in which you can either suggest or recommend to those that use Craigslist, in order for them to purchase the affiliate products that you are offering.

As there are so many people now turning to Craigslist in order to look for products and services that are being offered to them, then you should not miss out if you are looking for a way to earn a living from home through using the internet. All the users of this site are highly targeted (and already categorized for your convenience) and will be keen to find what it is that they want. So the sooner you get your Craigslist campaign under way, then the sooner you can start watching your profits climb.

Chapter 5

How to Post Your Advertisement on Craigslist

Posting your advertisement is really quite easy and straightforward to do. Plus, the other great thing is that any advert you do post here, unless it relates to a job listing (for certain major cities), it is free.

There are actually a couple of different ways in which you can post your adverts on to the site, and below we will take you through each one step by step.

First, you need to find the city you want to post your advert in. Actually finding your city, or the one in which you want to post your advert, is very easy indeed. On the right hand side of the page you will see the following list subdivided out as follows:-

- Countries

- States

- Cities

- Provinces

So, say for example you live in the United States, and then you just click on the state and the area which is closest to where you are. However, you may find that if you live in one of the major US cities, such as New York, Washington DC, Las Vegas etc., then it is probably already showing up on the home page of this site.

However if you live in another country, then finding the area that is closest to you is just as easy…just click on the country where you live, and then search through until you find a location that is close to where you reside.

The next step is where you need to find the category that you want to post your advert in. So if, for example, you want to place an ad in the small biz ads category, you will need to go into services, and then go to the link that says "sm biz ads" and click on it.

Now you have entered the category where you are interested in posting your advert, you need to click on the post link button. This link can be found in the top right hand corner of the page.

You will now be presented with a list of all the categories in the services section again, and you should immediately click on the link which says "small biz ads".

Once this has been clicked, you will find that you can actually start to post your ad. Below we will take a look at just how this looks.

1. Posting Title

This is required, and you should make it not only very descriptive, but also as catchy as possible.

You want to draw the attention of those using Craigslist to what you are offering. There are thousands of ads…make sure yours doesn't get lost in the sea!

2. Specific Location

Although you do not need to enter any information into this section if you do not want to, you should at least put in the area where you are located.

3. Price

This is located right next to the location box, and again it is up to you whether you enter any information into this or not.

4. Posting Description

This is where the main part of your advertisement is placed, and will tell those reading it what they will be getting, and the benefits they can gain from it. It all depends on what you are offering, and what your intentions are in relation to the ad that you have placed, as to how descriptive it is.

So if you happen to be selling a product, then it is best that you provide the best description possible to those reading the advert.

However, if you are just trying to get them to come to your own website, or to click on an affiliate link that you have, then maybe just providing them with a few teaser lines is the best option, and will get them going to your website in order to learn more about what you have to offer.

Again, be very careful using a technique like this, as it is something that *could* get you banned. Be creative, and find ways to work within the confines of the rules that Craigslist has in place.

The final part of the process of placing an advert on Craigslist is to input your email address. It is vital that you input an email address which you use regularly, and so will be checking on a regular basis. Also, make sure that the one you input is valid, because at the end of the process, Craigslist will send an email to you in order to finalize the listing that you have posted.

It is important to note that any postings you make will not go live until you have responded to the email sent from the site.

Adding Images

Not all categories allow you to add an image. For those that do, you will see that there is a button which says "Add/Edit Images".

By clicking on this link, you are then able to gain access to the locations on your computer where your images are stored, and find the one that is most appropriate to your posting.

By adding an image to your advert, you are potentially increasing the number of click through that your ad will receive. Even if you are just using a generic picture that you have obtained from your website, it is best if you post this as opposed to nothing at all.

Permissions Box

This box gives permission to others to contact you with regard to other commercial interests, products or services related to what you are offering. It is optional whether you allow others permission to contact you or not.

After completing all the sections above, you will then come to a button which says "continue". You need to click on this, as it will show you the advert you have just produced. It allows you to review it at this stage and make any changes to it.

If you do need to make any changes, then just click on the "Edit" button and carry out the alterations as you need to. As soon as you are satisfied with what you have produced, you then need to type in the verification code provided in the box below, and then click on the "continue" button again.

As soon as you have clicked this button, you will go on to the next page, where the terms and conditions relating to placement of ads, and below these are a 2 buttons. One asks you to "accept the terms of use" and the other asks whether you wish to "decline the terms of use". However, in order for your listing to be accepted, you must accept the terms and conditions of use button.

Upon clicking on this button you will then be taken to a page that asks you to check your email so that you may finalize the posting. So, as soon as you are able to, go to your email address (the one you provided at the beginning of the process) and by clicking on the link, it then allows you to either Post, Edit or Delete the listing that you have just entered.

By following the simple instructions provided in the email that has been sent to you, you will soon be on your way to placing your first advertisement, and then start to earn from using Craigslist in the future.

After a few minutes, your advert will then appear live on the site, and once you have done a few of these postings, you will start to wonder just what all the fuss was about in the beginning when you first started.

Conclusion

Certainly many people have now heard the name Craigslist, but they are still unsure as to just what this site can be used for.

However today, this site is now receiving over 4 billion page views each month, so there do seem to be some people who have a better understanding of what it is, and the types of services that it can offer.

Essentially, Craigslist is very similar in many ways to the classified sections of newspapers, where people are able to post or respond to advertisements within them.

However with Craigslist, a person is provided with a number of different advertisements, all online, and which can be found in various different categories, so it makes it much easier for those searching for information on products or services to find the advertisements that have been posted to it.

Today, many people are now using Craigslist as a way for them to earn either an additional salary, or as their main salary. They can do this through a number of different ways, but the main two we have been looking at through this book relates to:

1. Promoting a business.

2. Selling products or services on it.

In fact, in recent moves, Craigslist has become one of the most popular ways to date for a business, whether it is large or small, to promote itself. No matter the size of the business, each ad that they place (unless it happens to relate to a job) will be completely free of charge.

Any business owner can place their advertisement in the services section of Craigslist, and this section is then broken down into a number of different categories in order to allow them to place their advert in the most appropriate location, and the one in which it is likely to reach their target audience.

Although there is a small business section, it may well be worth your while placing your adverts in those categories which are best suited to what you are offering, rather than in a general category. By doing this, you are more likely to reach those people that are interested in what you have to offer.

It is also vital that you take part in discussion forums, as this is a great place where you can provide insightful information, and provide people with accurate responses to questions that they may have raised. It also allows you to provide a link in this section where you can then help to drive even more traffic to your website.

However, it is important that, when taking part in such forums, you avoid making your postings in such a way that people will look at them and think that they are spam (in other words, provide no use aside from blatant self promotion), which will simply steer them away from what you are trying to provide to them.

You may well find that those who mediate for Craigslist could well remove your posting from the site completely, and if they perceive that you are spamming too much, may remove you from being a subscriber to their services.

As well as being able to promote your business, the other way many people are now earning a profit from Craigslist is through selling items on it.

You are allowed to sell both new and used items through this site, and unlike with eBay, you can post a number of different items to it, and you will not be charged a single cent for posting them to this site.

As with eBay, this site allows you to post your items into various different categories, and allows you to supply a description of the item and how much it will cost to purchase. Plus, it also allows people to place adverts for items that they want, and again, these can be placed at no cost to you whatsoever.

However, when it comes to posting adverts for items for sale, there are some restrictions in place to those items which can not be sold through Craigslist. This includes firearms or pornographic items. Anyone trying to make their money in this way will soon find themselves on the wrong side of the law.

Craigslist works closely with law enforcement agencies of all types to help ensure that the site is not being used for illegal purposes.

Overall, if you are seriously considering ways of making a profit from running an online business, or are already running one and wish to expand, then it may well be worth your while taking a more in depth look at just what Craigslist can offer you.

Craigslist Money Making

www.ingramcontent.com/pod-product-compliance
Lightning Source LLC
Chambersburg PA
CBHW070728180526
45167CB00004B/1666